BACK PRINCIPLES:
A BOOK OF SPIRITUAL FATIGUE

Books by Stephen Bett

So Got Schooled: three memoirs

Un/Wired

The Gross & Fine Geography: New & Selected Poems

Those Godawful Streets of Man: a book of raw wire in

the city

Breathing Arizona: A Journal

Penny-Ante Poems: a book of break down

Sound Off: a book of jazz

Re-positioning

Track This: a book of relationship

S PLIT

Extreme Positions

Sass 'n Pass

Three Women

Nota Bene Poems: A Journey

High Maintenance

Trader Poets

High Design Refit

Cruise Control

Lucy Kent and other poems

BACK PRINCIPLES:
A BOOK OF SPIRITUAL FATIGUE

STEPHEN BETT

BLAZEVOX[BOOKS]
Buffalo, New York

Back Principles
A Book of Spiritual Fatigue
by Stephen Bett
Copyright © 2018

Published by BlazeVOX [books]

Printed in the United States of America

Interior design and typesetting by Geoffrey Gatza
Cover Art: Miles Lowry

First Edition
ISBN: 978-1-60964-310-2
Library of Congress Control Number: 2018932946

BlazeVOX [books]
131 Euclid Ave
Kenmore, NY 14217
Editor@blazevox.org

publisher of weird little books

BlazeVOX [books]

blazevox.org

21 20 19 18 17 16 15 14 13 12 01 02 03 04 05 06 07 08 09 10

BlazeVOX

Acknowledgments

Several of these poems have appeared in the following journals in Canada, the U.S., and England:

Boog City, Empty Mirror, Friday's Poems, North of Oxford, Orbis, Rasputin, Windsor Review, Ygdrasil

And thanks also to Phafours Press for the chapbook *though we are incredibly small for Katie, whose breath still brings love*

Table of Contents

BACK PRINCIPLES:
A BOOK OF SPIRITUAL FATIGUE

Back Principles (1) : you have my back

You have my back,
will teach me
buddhist principles
for non-fretting

If you *have* my
back, nothing
to fret
about
(non?)

But seriously,
even backs
have a learn
ing curve
     —none has
been bent to
break point
till now

You can heal it ...?

I am astonished

     —& begin

to believe you

(…yes)

Back Principles (2) : fret no more

You cover my back
with your hands,
probing, caressing,
easing, not just
fascia but life's
hard wear
& tear

You promise your
buddha love
will teach me
fret no
more

I will fall into
this feeling,
you will
catch me
          —pls
let me do
likewise &
not think
about it

No mind—
two hearts
two souls

Invisible spine
holds them
in correct
purposeful
line

Back Principles (3) : thru walls

I back into you
sorry it was on
purpose one of
those little
moments
desire compels

I would back into
you again & again
until you reach
out for me—
then never stop
backing up

I would back thru
long walls with
you, in fact
maybe we're
already doing
so …?

Back Principles (4) : in healthful tune

Your back is to
me & I hold
you, hold
onto you
& hear your
body say
yes, this is
the right
way

You have yet
to say 'maybe'
to me, nor
I you

We go from
somewhat
fretful
'yes'
        (for god
buddha sake)
to simple
(outrageous)
'yes pls'

fretless
musician-
speak,
this is in
healthful
tune

Back Principles (5) : naked air / stunned emptiness

You teach me more
than all that is
behind my back
(years, decades
since)

I have learned
nothing till you
came into my
charred world
(burn the spine-
bound books,
their fraught
lives)

I learn to lean
back simply
into naked air,
all that holds
me up

You have opened
this stunned

emptiness,
this air that
tests my
back

Back Principles (6) : I am still afraid

I am still afraid
of losing you
dying with-
out you

Now we *have*
our backs it
is horror to
free-fall
alone into
our last
journeys

You say you
will teach me
letting go is
buddha love
—can anyone
be so certain
or so strong

I know you
are here for

life's edge

I will lean
against air,
but a void …?

There is no
back word
here, no
backbone

This is a path
we all struggle
on (a back-
road?)
          —no
"I found its"
on the way,
no instant
grass-i-ass

Just endless
wrestling
in the mud
with angels

Of whom you
would be
cleanly mine,
surely

Back Principles (7) : be blessed for that

I will *try* to learn
what you teach me

… difficult student

Confused, full
of doubt
(all sides,
paths)

Guilt is *not*
the issue

It is the holy desire
to believe (say
it was Heysus
of Nazareth)
on the back
side of
liturgy,
built on
lies (& its

history)

Is your Buddha
different?

Your strength
lies somewhere
(beyond any
doubt)

Let it have
my back, &
be blessed
for that

Back Principles (8) : it must live in us

You *have* my back

Let that be blessing
enough

(More than I
am worth …)

Let me be worthy
to have yours

There is nothing
else we can do

You know more
than I, which is
little enough

Hold each other
—front-word &

back-word,
now till
eternity

This is the
blessing,
yours &
mine

It must live
in us

No-where else
to go

No-where else
at all likely
to go

Back to
back …

How else to
travel

And with whom

It can only
be done this
way

Get ready

Back Principles (10) : forward / gone

Do not fret, she
goes with you

That is the way
forward, when
all else has
stumbled
hopelessly
sideways

Too much, too
many times
never looking
careful enough
ahead, ground,
guidelines
(or guides)

She alone has
your back
(ever)
         —trust

& rejoice you

fickle, duped
stumblebum
your days are
gloriously
(outrageously)
numbered
now

One, two,
three
gone

Back Principles (11) : fretless music

She gives you
the buddha
you hold the
christ

Fretless music

Back to back

Do *not* prosthletize
evangelize
(ticky-tacky)

The brain learns
heart, needs
no washing

Back Principles (12) : doesn't speak words

You follow her call
down this path

No-one has ever said
follow me

Tired of leading
nowhere ...

Trust is the
option left

The footing will
be *where*
it is

My guide is
my wisdom

  —& she
doesn't speak
words

Back Principles (13) : doesn't mouth words

She doesn't mouth
words either

She looks in
my eyes …

Back Principles (14) : Keats & Rilke coming up again (& damned Spicer, too)

Who sees into me
… has mine heart?

Too easily tossed
(on a heap, on
a mound)

This inning is
future time
(grace time …?)

I would take
a pitcher
of you

Drink it, bat it
out of here
—whatever
it takes

I lose myself
completely, am
struck dumb
in your
buddha
love

Where is my
ground, where
is my Heysus
spinning to
now

This (heady) gain
is nerve loss
(also)

It is mystery
one enters
—terrified
(& possibly
alive …)
Witless &
spooked,
& unafraid
to say so

(god help
me)

Look in mine
eyes & give
me your
strength,
I have none
that doesn't
shake the bases
loose in the
night

Look in mine
eyes, I have
forgotten how
to see

Back Principles (15) : the Cradle

Why do I keep
coming back to these
un-manageable things,
images
         —they mean
nothing
(to me)

They have history
on their side
which means
what, exactly
—that they
are images,
cradles we
put things in
till later
(all our lives)

They are just
open hoarding
drawers

Do they have our
backs up to
& including
the big un-lock

Do we shake them out
anywhere after-
wards

We are civilized
people, but
have no real
homes at all
        —empty
cradles

Back Principles (16) : won't be budged

Ok I won't fret
the small stuff

—still leaves the big
one (that locker …
fret-full, yaah)

That last closed
drawer

Scares the be-jesus
(hey Zeus)
out of me, & isn't
bravado always
the biggest liar
of all

What if it won't
go, it's never
gone anywhere
anyway

Won't be budged

Locked in for
life, sitting
in a cradle
staring out
at me

Back Principles (17) : endless drawers

Maybe when you get
tired of looking at
it (& it you)
that's when you
can just walk
away

Give up all the
ghosts
      —yours
& everyone
else's

See your life
pass before
your eyes

Wish you knew
where it was
going

Or not …
(oh that
drawer
again …)

Endless

Back Principles (18) full on / full off

It's like roulette for
methuselurities

Drawers opening
& closing
without end

Nightmare either
way
  —full on
or *full off*

Beyond terror

Give me the
Nazarene, pls

Shut the casino
rip out the gaudy
red carpeting,
dim the flakey

lights

Keep something else
dimly burning
for a while
(god sake
on that,
buddha
too)

Back Principles (19) : sapien & cowardly heart

Been through the agoraphobic's
desert, Yuma at 117 degrees

Life in the furnace under
a terrifying open sky
(no place to burrow)

You say I need to en-
dure the sweat-lodge,
sleep with snakes
& scorpions
at my side
(every fear alive)

Live a full week
w/ the Terrors
(find the buddha …
or the christ
magnified?)

You say …
you say …

And in you I
surely trust
(god help
me ...)

True soul
touch me,
ease me
(somewhat ...)

Horror wherein lurks
the desert of my
sapien &
cowardly
heart

Back Principles (20) : unremarkable things

Burrow into fear
it is no simple
exercise

Comes nearer (& dearer)
each moment you are ā-
way, indistractible

Will not rest when
you are on that
wild, ridiculous
sky-road to
habitats un-
known
        —will not
rest, habituated
or no

There *is* no rest
for the wicked
(of course)
nor for the brave
(space-rider)

So do not be brave
it means nothing
at all

Poseurs & bravado

Live in fear (or quest)
of the buddha &
the christ
            —fretless,
back to back

Spineless & ā-feared
(endlessly, & to
no good)

Six string or twelve?
(he fretted)

My christ I cannot
do that, it is no
sacred thing

(hanging on metal
or on nylon
strings)

It is a string (a loop)
of unmerited, un-
remarkable
things

I was hanging in
there, waiting,
noting your
admirable lack
of fear
(grace notes)

Synapses or some-
thing real, like
slide guitar,
hard wired
straight to
the spun
down
soul

I beg you christ-
like, & you
slide by un-
noticed

Back Principles (21) : out of your hands

You teach me & I
am stubborn,
go stubborn in
your hands

I am dumb,
ā-feared

And yet,
knowing
you …

I could be …
could just
be

But that is
so far to
go

A life-time trying
to think it
through

You're right, I
am nowhere

(And nowhere
to be found)

Letting go carries
all the fear out
of your
hands

I would be
braced in
you
(or wish
to be)

Loop your fingers
together (pls)
& catch me

Make a brace
that holds
the *two*
of us

For eternity …

A brace
that nets
the both
of us
too

Back Principles (22) : naked

This is naked
(I know)
but it be not
cheap

It is spare &
minimal
(as you
would
wish
me)

I live in your
shadow &
you ask nothing
of me but
let go

This is the least
you can teach
me, give
myself
to me

Naked &
no easy
thing

And forever
running out
of time to
learn

Back Principles (23) : ready to pay

Running down the
clock, see the
naked man
run

All his bounded
glory absenting
itself
—you call for
a U-turn

Illegal on this high-
way
         he points out
signage
(stickler for
detail)

Go with your lips
stuck closed then
they don't bother
with a seal
(nor a kiss)

They have you in
the thought loop
want you un-
prepared for
closure,
ready to
pay

Back Principles (24) : in absence

Spiritual crises a life-
time, & virgin births
dime a dozen

Spiritual crisis
parables by
committee &
a lost Q

Mis-translations
mis-dating
mis-placing
gā-lore

And yet the christ
sits still
(like your buddha)
        —resonant
as all
desire

Tormenting in
absence

Back Principles (25) : make it land

Tonight we are both
in pain (space-rider)

Back to back
we can only
stand
(webbed
netted
braced)

I will hold you
it is just
return

There is another
"principle" here
—if we can
find it …

But it *is*
here

Lives inside
        … your
buddha, his
christ,
who knows
for sure …

It is not a
dead thing,
it can fly
(space-rider)

Watch it …

… come & go

One day, pls,
make it
land

Back Principles (26) : this agoraphobic thing

He would fly to you
again tonite if
he could

On the wings
of a Q

On a hope
that it be
true

Far easier
to believe
in you …

This is the
struggle
(of course)

Struggle path, back-
road, wrestle ground

(muddied
angels)

Welcome to the
sweat-lodge

The furnace is
set at 117,
& going
higher

Hang on to
the nearest
nylon string,
you won't like
this agora-
phobic
thing

Back Principles (27) : things that cowards say

She is burning by the
sweat-lodge, burn-
ing, flaming out

He's watching thru
his open drawer,
surprised to see
fire & smoke
pass by all
holy doubt

Monks will kerosene
themselves alight
(unafraid entire
vast night)

He will squint
liquid eyes all
morning long,
watch her return
comes on strong

We are not monks,
he said (did dis-
avow)
enough sweat
already on my
naked brow

Oh the things
that cowards
say
        when
she is still so
far away

Back Principles (28) : watching you breathe

You will bring your
buddha back
on your return

That will mean
nothing &
everything
to him

Night chills will be
stuck back in
the drawer
(until un-
locked
again)

He would have
you teach him
(alone)
     just by
watching you
breathe

He would have
you near, help
him choose be-
tween the two

Wiser still, he
would include
himself,
three at least
by now

(And you make
four)

So where does he
go after you?

Too many questions
—just silence
for response

Hold on, hold\
on to each\
other is all\
they can\
think\
to do

And that forever\
temporary too

Back Principles (30) : absent there

This suddenly isn't working
out too well (he read
himself between
the lines)

Maybe no-one has
anyone's back
at all (after
all, at all—
that kind of
small 'n all)

Maybe it's just
something to yab
about until the
light goes out

There are no bones
or backbones then,
nothing holding
any of it up

Except the weak
promise of
tomorrow's
breath of
air

And your buddha
seems sublimely
absent there

Back Principles (31) : make some fizz

Absent tarmac, rails
roads, you can't
travel *to* it

Not a place on
the map, try
inside she
said

Too glib? (Or fib …)
And how get
there any-
way? Bore a
hole, you
bore ("to
himself")

Nothing ever
works the way
advertised,
why should
spirits move in
there now ?

There is hot &
there is cold
(another one just
flew by)

Can't bore a hole
in cold sky, try
your backbone,
make some fizz

Back Principles (32) : all the way to hell

Heading south
inside himself
—to touch
the christ

Much help
needed
(of, or off,
course)

Navigate
too much
bones in
the way

Sinew too

The christ is
silent
(buddha too)
—means nothing
at all, nothing

new

You gotta
reach
deeper
or not
at all

Wring the
bowel next,
like a door-
bell
… all the way
to hell (&
gone)

Back Principles (33) : continuously greased

Nothing more to report
at present, the usual
static in way of
penetration heart
or soul, whichever
makes more sense
in these terrifying
&/or godforsaken
moments &
glimpses
of true
time

Nothing new in the
sweat locker &
same lock on
the perennial
drawer

The medieval drawer
slid easy to & fro
being so
continuously &
smoothly
greased

Back Principles (34) : spiritual fatigue

This is surely
spiritual fatigue
(on the loose)
(at loose ends)

Backed into a corner
(loosely speaking)

Back me, back
me not …

My back is knotted

Lies bound in a
locked drawer

When it creaks open
pray for something
merciful

Pray there is
something
there

You will not
have my back
beyond this
point

It will be loose
at ease, or it
will be
broken

Back Principles (35) : genealogy

Going in deep
(by now)
need rimes
w/ fatigue

Is (surely) driving
this path
(muddied
angels, ruts
& all)

Where does this
genealogy
"get off" ?
(the beaten
track one
lies in)

We've been
"all over it"
endlessly
by now—
sliding

drawer

Our live-sprung
young ones—
where are we
from ?

We're "at"
where do
we *go*
from
here ?

Back Principles (36) : them who need

We "go" to darkness
(or to light …)

Pray the christ
(baldly bold
here)
will "be" there
after all

It is (finally)
our cultural
in-heritance
(genealogy)

The buddha
in another's
drawer

Bless them all

That seek …

Bless his love
(who sees the
buddha)

Bless him who
yearns to see

Bless them
who need

Back Principles (37) : blessings

Bless him
—for he
needs

His need
grows
yearly
(mouldy crop
on a side-
path)

She cures it
(kindness of
her buddha)

But not his
(not his)
(knotted up)

He asks the
christ …
hiding

in his
drawer

That now ungreased
static-y slide,
that *leap*
of faith

I slide by you
un-noticed in
your temple,
bless you
(who have
found)

Bless me
(who has
need of
you)

Back Principles (38) : (truthfully) alone / Behind you

I leap
you (singular) leap
he, she, or it leaps

I was leaping

I shall have leaped (leapt?)
(like a damned leper ...)

I am leaping
(all ways)

She (you) give him
courage
to leap
(unashamed)

Out of the
(spirit) closet,
the drawer

For the christ

God help him …

His need
is naked
& (truthfully)
alone

Behind you

Back Principles (39) : pockets empty

Yes, we have each
other's back
… till death
do us part

I have no other
"principles"
left

Back left & back
right pockets
sitting on
empty

Back Principles (40) : as you do

How can he love
the christ
when *you* are
so there, so
very there
(for him)

And your buddha
cannot speak
to him …

As you do

Back Principles (41) : how to go forward

Path to the Divine
(is the christ)

How he thinks …

But now *you* –
path to the
path

(Tao to Tao ?)

I feel you
behind me

Still not knowing
how to go
forward
(without
you)

Back Principles (42) : so *incredibly* small

This is crazy-mazy talk,
one of those wonky
prayer paths,
Thesean

Goes in circles too

Comes (always)
back to you

Perhaps the christ
is in the buddha

The buddha in
the christ

We are so
incredibly
small,
we'd fit in
anything
at all

Back Principles (43) : she said so too

Why so afraid
it's only a
flippin'
drawer

Closes & locks
down easy
some fine
one day

(After a lot
of thought)

The drawer is
well versed
in this,
you're not
(that's the rub)

And thinking
doesn't help

(She said so
too, &
said the
buddha
knew)

Back Principles (44) : another lifetime

Ok, he'd almost come
to say, let's
get this over
with …

Let's shut the god-
damn drawer

Then you came along,
wedged it wide again

There are two paths
to this chest,
forward
& back
(two beats)

Go back then,
put it off
another life-
time

Do this for me,
he said
(pls believe
him, & those
who follow)

Back Principles (45) : all we can do

This doesn't solve
anything, just
delays it

But what a
way to go
out
(make it
last life-
times
two)

You finally
at his back

Prayer is pure
selfishness
(leave the
christ, the
buddha
well enough
alone)

I pray to you …

Let me have
your back
too

(All we can
do)

Back Principles (46) : feel my face open

This is not over

The search
spirituelle

And for love
(just the once)

There *is* a
connection
(though it
baffles)

Two-three-four-
cornered
god …

And you
—at my
back

And before
me ...

Feel my
face
open

Back Principles (47) : the christ, the buddha, & you (love)

You
you
& you

(god …)

You, you & you

Where do
we go
from
here ?

Back Principles (48) : seal it in your soul

Where do we go
from here, where
did we go
from here

"Arrivals" is at
5:00 p.m.
(local time)

Take me some-
where then

Take him …

Take them both
home

Let the christ
find them
there,
waiting

Ask your
buddha
to do this
for you

Then seal it
in your
soul

Back Principles (49) : nothing left to do

You have brought him
closer to the christ
than anyone
has before

And you follow
the buddha (!)

He would bleed
for you, give
his life for
you

Look what you
have *done*

It is miracle
enough

Nothing left
to do but
wait …

Back Principles (50) : with you too

I wait
you wait
he, she, or it waits

No—— you have
found

I wait alone
(but with you)

He waits alone
(with you too)

Back Principles (51) : think big

Put this thing off
keep the drawer
open, you wedge
it there

He would bleed
inside, or
without

You know that …

He is not ready
to leave you

Yet you have
brought him
to this place

You (she)
him (me)

Bless you …

We are incredibly
small for this

The christ, the
buddha, makes
us think
big

Back Principles (52) : agoraphobic

Big spaces are
made of this

Phoenix to Yuma
—terrifying

The christ to
the buddha …
terrifying too

Hold my back (pls)
the landscape
would break
it in halves

Agoraphobic,
big space

Holding emptiness
in my hands

Back Principles (53) : face the christ / thank your buddha well

He would hold
only you

Only you
will do

Then he nears
the christ

Broken hands
may heal

Touch & time

Let there be
enough of
each

You will heal

this

That is the
"leap" of
faith

The rest will
take care of
itself

Then he'll face
the christ
(& thank
your
buddha
well)

Back Principles (54) : all over his face

Bring us together

Brought us
together
(… yes)

There is a
promise
here

It is made,
sealed

We breathe it

You breathe
yours, he
breathes
his

You make
it true

Bring it, deliver
it over,
your breath
all over
his face

Back Principles (55) : like the wind

The buddha in
your breath

Stirs the christ
in his soul

Remember
that …

Like the wind
on his face
as a child

Never forgotten

It must
be so,
he feels
it still

Your breath
reminds
him

And the christ
(& the buddha)
were there

Back Principles (56) : if you will

Let go, she says,
stop thinking …

Fall into your
buddha

Call him the
christ, if
you will

Back Principles (57) : no meaning

He will have
your back
too

When you
fall

Know this …

No matter
the name

Words have
no meaning
here (at all)

Back Principles (58) : more than life itself

Your breath like some
kind of long
remembered
wind on his
face

Shake him closer
than ever

The christ love
& buddha love
are one

Get him there

You say to him
I love you more
than life itself

It is miracle
enough

The Divine lives
here, call it
what you will

Though we are in-
credibly small
the path just
got shorter
by two
breaths

Back Principles (59) : you make this journey

Life itself …
life itself

What better path
(or place)

Mud washes off,
drawers open
close en route

You make this
journey cleaner
(clearer)
from terrified
space

Back Principles (60) : befriend them on their ancient way

This is as close as
we can (possibly)
come, the gift
of our lives

Miracle enough

The path has
two backs
to carry it

They *have*
each other's
back

No matter what
muddied angels
say

The buddha &
the christ
befriend them
on their
ancient
way

STEPHEN BETT is a widely and internationally published Canadian poet. His earlier work is known for its *sassy, edgy, hip…* *caustic wit*—indeed, for the *askance look* of the *serious satirist… skewering* what he calls the 'vapid monoculture' of our times. His more recent books have been called *an incredible accomplishment* for their *authentic minimalist* subtlety. Many are tightly sequenced book-length 'serial' poems, which allow for a rich echoing of cadence and image, building a *wonderfully subtle, nuanced music*.
Bett follows in the avant tradition of Don Allen's *New American Poets*. Hence the mandate for Simon Fraser University's "Contemporary Literature Collection" to purchase and archive his "personal papers" for scholarly use. He is recently retired after a 31-year teaching career largely at Langara College in Vancouver, and now lives with his wife Katie in Victoria, BC. For reviews of all his books, and for recent interviews, see www.stephenbett.com

Made in the USA
Monee, IL
07 July 2026

56551501R00072